Lane Memorial Library

3 4509 00133308 7

D1509386

10-00

Lane Memorial Library
2 Academy Avenue
Hampton NH 03842-2280

Lane Memorial Library
2 Academy Avenue
Hampton NH 03842-2280

EXPERIMENTS WITH
FLIGHT

EXPERIMENTS WITH FLIGHT

Frank McCormick

CHERRY TREE BOOKS

A Cherrytree Book

Designed and produced by
Pemberton Press Ltd

First published 1992
by Cherrytree Press Ltd
a subsidiary of
The Chivers Company Ltd
Windsor Bridge Road
Bath, Avon BA2 3AX

Copyright © Cherrytree Press Ltd 1992

British Library Cataloguing in Publication Data

McCormick, Frank
  Experiments with Flight.
  1. Science. Experiments using floating objects
  I. Title II. Series
  507.24

  ISBN 0-7451-5116-7

All rights reserved. No part of this publication may be reproduced, stored
in a retrieval system, or transmitted. in any form or by any means
without the prior permission in writing of the publisher, nor be otherwise
circulated in any form of binding or cover other than that in which it is
published and without a similar condition including this condition being
imposed on the subsequent purchaser.

Contents

Principles of Flight

Flying Machines

Getting Started

Before you do any experiments, take a few minutes to read the Safety Notes on page 42 at the back of the book. None of these experiments is dangerous, but you will need to be careful in handling some of the household items. If you read something that is not clear to you, or if you have any questions about an experiment, ask an adult or an older friend for some help.

Some of the experiments have a marker that looks like this:

This means that you should ask permission to do the experiment. You may need help from an adult.

DO NOT do experiments marked

unless an adult is available to help you.

In all of the experiments, try to follow the directions as closely as possible. For the experiments in which you need to make something, the drawings will help you understand more about the things you are building. Most of the experiments will work better if you follow the drawings as closely as you can. If an experiment doesn't work first time, try to work out why and then try again.

Principles of Flight

People have dreamed about flying for thousands of years. How lucky we are now that flying is real. Jet aeroplanes take us on holiday and deliver fresh foods all over the world. Hospitals can move patients by helicopter when treatment is needed quickly. Satellites and space shuttles let us watch Earth's crops and weather from outer space. Many people fly small aircraft for fun. Can you think of other ways that flying makes our lives better?

This book will help you understand many of the principles that make flight possible. There are four basic forces that act on all flying objects. These forces are called lift, drag, thrust and gravity. You can do experiments designed to show how they behave. Then you will be able to understand and explain the flying machines described in the second part of the book.

Gravity

Gravity is the force that makes things fall to Earth. No matter how high you hit a tennis ball, it always comes back down. If you slip on an icy pavement in the winter, you fall to the ground. Gravity pulls on everything and everybody.

Falling together

If you drop an object, it will fall straight down. Every object, whether heavy or light, will fall down at the same speed. A marble would fall beside an elephant if you could drop them together. Some people still believe that heavy things fall faster. You can show that heavier things fall at the same speed as lighter ones.

You will need
a new bar of soap, still in
  the wrapper
an old paperback book
a small cushion
a pillow
an empty plastic bottle
a shoe
a soft toy
a large paper clip
a pencil
a rubber

1. Hold one of the objects listed here in each hand. Drop them at the same time from the same height on to a bed or the carpet.

2. Notice that they always hit the bed or the floor at the same time.

3. Try this experiment with other pairs of objects.

Falling fast and slow

The things you dropped didn't have far to fall. If you could drop them from a great height, they would hit the ground at different times. This does not mean that the previous experiment was wrong. Gravity really does affect everything in the same way. But something else happens. The force of the air on an object affects it during its fall.

1. Crumple one piece of paper into a tight ball.

2. Hold the crumpled paper over your head in one hand. In the other, hold the flat sheet of paper.

3. Let both of them go at the same time. Which always hits the ground first?

You will need
2 pieces of A4 paper

The two pieces of paper are trying to fall together (because of gravity). But when any object falls, it traps air beneath it. This trapped air pushes up on the falling object. That makes the object fall more slowly. The larger the surface, and the lighter the object, the more air it will trap, so the more upward push it will feel.

Thrust

All aeroplanes with engines and all rockets depend on thrust. Thrust makes them move forward. They push large amounts of air or other gases in one direction. This makes the aircraft fly in the other direction. You can see how thrust works in these experiments with balloons.

You will need
1 long balloon
heavy paper
tape
felt-tipped pens

Uncontrolled flight
1. Use felt-tipped pens to decorate the balloon as an aeroplane if you like. It is easier to draw on the balloon if you blow it up first. Do not tie it shut. Tie it round a matchstick or a pencil.

2. Cut wings from the heavy paper. Tape them to the centre top of the "plane".

3. Remove the matchstick or pencil. Blow the balloon up as full as you can. Let it go. Thrust will make it fly around the room in a series of loops and turns until it runs out of air.

Controlled flight

Now see if you can control the balloon's flight.

1. Cut two 7·5cm (3in) pieces of straw. Thread them on to the string.

2. Tie each end of the string to chairs or other pieces of furniture.

3. Blow up the balloon. Tie it round a matchstick or a pencil.

You will need
1 long balloon
3m (10ft) of thin string
 or heavy button thread
1 plastic drinking straw
masking tape
felt-tipped pens

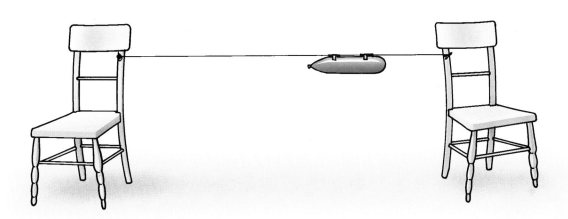

4. Tape the balloon securely to the straw as shown.

5. Move the balloon to the end of the string. Remove the matchstick or pencil and let the balloon go. Thrust will push it to the other end.

You can do this experiment outdoors if you like. Tie the string to strong sticks or canes stuck in the ground. You can do lots of experiments. Use strings of different lengths and balloons of different sizes and shapes. Have races with your friends to see which shapes work best.

Drag

When a parachute begins to fall, air rushes into the "umbrella" part, which is called the "canopy". As the canopy fills with air, it spreads out and traps even more air. This trapped air pushes up against the parachute. The trapped air causes it to fall much more slowly. The force that slows the parachute down is called drag. Drag acts on everything that moves, including things that fly.

You will need

a large handkerchief or square scarf
4 pieces of string, each 45cm (18in) long
a toy figure or small weight
plastic sheet
tissue paper
tape

1. Tie a piece of string 45cm (18in) long to each corner of a large handkerchief.

2. Gather up the four free ends of the strings, and tie them to a small toy figure or to a weight such as a large metal washer.

3. Stand over the stairs or on a chair. Hold the parachute by the centre of the canopy and drop it. The parachute will inflate immediately and fall gently to the floor.

Venting the canopy

Drop your parachute from as great a height as you can safely manage. Watch how it falls. Can you see how the canopy rocks from side to side? Real parachutes have a special hole cut in the top of the canopy to stop the rocking. This hole is called a "vent". The vent helps to reduce drag. Cut a tiny vent hole in the centre of your canopy. Drop it again. Does it still rock? If it does, make the vent slightly larger.

Air Pressure and Lift

Everything is made of molecules. The molecules in solids, like wood, are close together. In a gas, like air, they are much further apart. Air molecules are constantly on the move. They bang into any surface exposed to the air. So the air is actually pushing against those surfaces.

You can use air to make things move, just as the wind can blow dry leaves across your garden or make the blades of a windmill go round. The force of air that makes objects move upwards is called "lift". The flight of birds and aircraft would be impossible without lift.

Lift a strip of paper with no hands

About 250 years ago, a Swiss mathematician called Daniel Bernoulli discovered that the faster the air moves, the more its pressure drops. He also found that when air moves over a surface, the pressure of the air on that surface is reduced. You can see this effect in the following experiment.

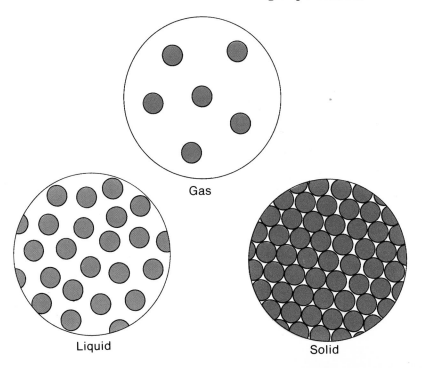

Gas

Liquid

Solid

1. Hold a piece of paper by the corners of one edge. Bring it up to your mouth. The paper will droop towards the floor.

2. Blow gently across the top surface of the paper. Does the paper still droop or does it rise slightly?

You will need
a piece of paper

3. Take a deep breath, and blow harder. What happens to the paper?

The paper moves only when the air pressure on one side is different from the pressure on the other side. Before you blow, the air on both sides of the paper is still. The air pressure is the same on both sides. When you blow over the upper surface, the pressure on that side is reduced. But the pressure underneath is the same as before. The higher pressure underneath forces the paper up. Blowing harder reduces the pressure on the upper surface even more. This makes the paper rise even higher.

Make money hop

Differences in air pressure can be great. They can lift metal objects – even heavy ones.

You will need
a coin
a paper plate
felt-tipped markers
  (optional)

1. Place the coin near the edge of a table. Put the paper plate 10-15cm (4-6in) behind it.

2. Hold your mouth just above the edge of the table. Blow hard over the top of the coin in one short, sharp blast. What happens?

By blowing over the coin, you reduce the air pressure above it. The higher pressure below the coin forces it to rise. After a few practice tries, you can make this happen every time. You can challenge your friends to a contest. Draw a target on the paper plate. See if you can make the coin land on the bull's-eye!

Lifting books with air

Can you lift a stack of books without touching them? Try this experiment and see. Remember to keep plastic bags away from small children!

1. Use a large plastic carrier bag or a small bin liner. Make sure that there are no holes in it.

2. Place the bag on the end of a table with the open end hanging over the edge.

3. Gather up the open end of the bag in your hand. Place several large books on top of the flattened bag. Keep holding the open end.

4. Make a small opening through your hand at the open end of the bag.

5. Blow into the bag through this small hole.

You will need

1 plastic bag
several books

The bag will fill with air, and the books will rise. You are forcing air into a confined space. The air inside the bag pushes in all directions. It pushes upwards against the books. This upward push is strong enough to overcome the weight of the books – the force of gravity.

Don't rush. If you feel dizzy, stop blowing. Squeeze the hole shut, and breathe normally for a few moments. Start blowing again whenever you feel like it.

Keep a ball in the air

Sometimes table tennis balls don't go where you think they will. You can trap one inside a stream of air, even when it looks as though there is nothing to hold the ball there.

The pipe

1. Place a table tennis ball over the end of a bubble pipe.

2. Take a deep breath through your nose. Blow steadily through the pipe.

You will need

1 table tennis ball
1 bubble pipe

Did the ball rise from the end of the pipe? It should rise and bob slightly in the stream of air. You'll soon see how to control the ball by blowing. Then you can walk around slowly without losing the ball.

The funnel

1. Hold the funnel upright. Rest the table tennis ball inside.

2. Tilt your head back so you can blow into the small end of the funnel.

3. Blow as hard as you can. Can you blow the ball out of the funnel?

4. Now take another deep breath. Blow hard, but this time turn the funnel upside down as you blow. Does the ball fall out? What happens when you stop blowing?

You will need
1 table tennis ball
1 funnel
a reversible vacuum
  cleaner

You can also control the ball continuously. Use a vacuum cleaner with a hose attachment that can blow air out as well as pulling air in. Place the small end of the funnel in the end of the hose and put the ball in the funnel. Hold the funnel tightly against the end of the hose with your hand. Set the vacuum cleaner to blow air out of the funnel. Entertain yourself and your friends with the unusual antics of a table tennis ball that defies gravity!

Blow things together

Can you explain why this experiment works the way it does?

You will need

2 table tennis balls
2 pieces of string, each
about 40cm (16in) long
masking tape
a straw

1. Tape a table tennis ball to one end of one of the strings. Tape the other end of the string to the edge of a table. Do the same with the other string and the second ball. The two balls should hang next to each other about 1cm (½in) apart.

2. Use a straw to blow gently between the two balls. What happens?

Follow-that-car balloon

Helium is a gas that is lighter than air. Balloons filled with it have to be tethered to stop them from floating away.

1. Pick a time when you are going for a ride in the car.

2. Close all of the windows and air vents in the car. Tape the free end of the balloon's string to the floor in the rear of the car. (Make sure the driver can still see in all directions.) The balloon should float near the ceiling but should be able to move freely.

3. Hold the balloon still when the car is stopped, then let it go as the car moves off. What happens when the car accelerates or goes round corners and bends?

You will need
a helium-filled balloon
masking tape

When the car starts to move forward, you are pressed back in your seat, but the balloon leans forward. The air in the car is also "pressed back" to the rear. This makes the air in the rear of the car slightly thicker. Thicker air means higher pressure. The higher pressure behind the balloon pushes it forwards.

The same thing happens on curves. Air piles up towards the outside of the turn, and the balloon is pushed to the inside.

Fill a jar with air
Can you move air from one jar to another?

You will need
2 plastic jars or glasses
a large bowl or bucket
of water

1. Fill the bowl with water or use the kitchen sink.

2. Lower the jars into the water. Hold one upside down. Hold the other one sideways. The upside-down jar should stay filled with air. What happens to the other one?

3. Turn the second jar – still filled with water – upside down. Hold the mouth of the air-filled jar just underneath it and to one side.

4. Tilt the mouth of the first jar towards the second. Watch as air bubbles rush to the top of the water-filled jar. These bubbles make a pocket of air in the top of the second jar. The air pushes the water in the second jar out into the bowl.

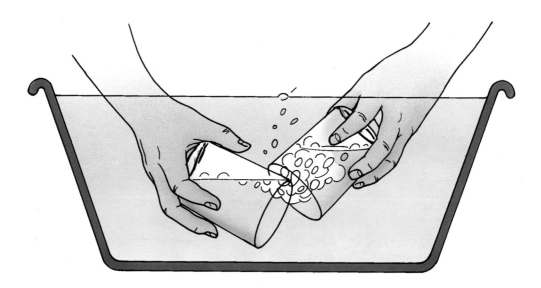

The hovercard

A cotton reel and a drawing pin can make a piece of card float on air.

1. Make sure the card is a true square. Draw diagonal lines across from corner to corner to find the centre of the card.

2. Push the drawing pin carefully through the card's centre.

3. Hold one end of the cotton reel close to your mouth. Hold the card against the other end of the reel, with the point of the pin inside the hole of the cotton reel.

4. Blow hard through the hole and let go of the card. What happens? What happens when you stop blowing?

You will need

a large solid wooden or plastic cotton reel
a 7.5cm (3in) square of thin card
a pencil and ruler
scissors
a drawing pin

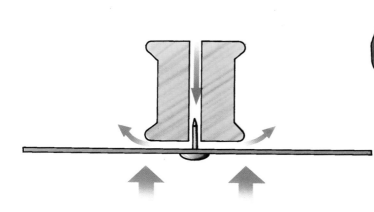

This experiment is like the ones you did with the funnel and table tennis ball. The air you blow through the cotton reel rushes out between the reel and the card. Air moving along a surface always reduces the pressure on that surface. In this experiment, when you blow, you reduce the pressure on the reel side of the card. The air pressure on the other side of the card remains the same, which keeps the card tight against the reel.

Make a plane wing

Aeroplane wings have a special shape that lets them create lift.

You will need
a sheet of paper
scissors
tape
ruler

1. Fold a piece of paper over on itself so that one side is about 2·5cm (1in) longer that the other. Crease the fold neatly and cut along the crease.

2. Take the larger piece of paper, and fold 1cm (½in) of the cut edge over. Crease it down.

3. Place the cut edge of the smaller piece of paper into the fold you have just made. Tape the two pieces together. The fold will be the front of your wing.

4. Tape the two free edges of the papers together to form the back edge of your wing. The upper piece of paper will be longer. It will be curved. The lower surface should remain flat.

5. Slide the ruler into the front edge.

6. Blow directly on the front edge so that air goes over both the top and the bottom of the wing. The wing should rise as the airstream generates lift.

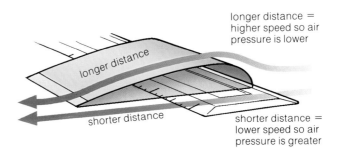

longer distance = higher speed so air pressure is lower

longer distance

shorter distance

shorter distance = lower speed so air pressure is greater

The air going over the curved top travels a greater distance. So it must travel faster than the air going underneath. The air moves more quickly over the top of the wing. This reduces the pressure on the upper surface, and the wing rises.

Flying Machines

Some machines, such as aeroplanes and rockets, need lots of power to fly great distances. Others, such as hot-air balloons and gliders move along quite nicely without their own power. Sometimes even a machine with several engines can act as if it has no engines at all. For example, a giant jumbo jet flying 11km (7mi) high could shut off all of its engines and still glide safely for quite a long way.

Hot-air Balloon

Warm air rises. If you can trap some warm air in a lightweight bag, the bag will rise, too.

You will need

a plastic dry-cleaner's bag
heavy art paper
compasses (for drawing
    circles)
scissors
tape
a canister-type
    vacuum cleaner

1. Ask a dry cleaner for a plastic cleaner's bag. Make sure it has no holes or tears in it. Tape the top hole in the bag shut.

2. Draw a circle on heavy paper about 15-20cm (6-8in) in diameter. Draw another circle about 1cm (½in) inside the first one. Cut out the circle into a ring. Tape the bottom edge of the plastic bag evenly round the ring.

3. Turn on the vacuum cleaner, and let it warm up.

4. Fill the plastic bag with the warm air from the vacuum cleaner. Let go of the bag. It will float gently away.

Kites

Go outdoors and let the wind provide lift for this experiment.

1. Cut 3 pieces of string, each 30cm (12in) long. Tie one end of each string to a small plastic button. Punch small holes in the food tray as shown and thread the strings through.

2. Tie the free ends of the strings together.

3. The tray is your kite. Make a tail for it with a piece of string 1m (3ft) long. Tie on 8 or 10 brightly coloured bows of crepe paper.

4. Attach the tail to the button at the bottom end of your kite.

5. Tie a long thin string to the knot you made in Step 2 above.

On a day with some wind, launch your kite. See how high you can make it fly. Try different lengths of tail. Does changing the tail make the kite fly better?

You will need

3 plastic buttons
a polystyrene food tray
crepe paper
a ball of thin string many
  metres long

Paper Planes

The same paper aeroplane can fly in many different ways.

You will need
a piece of A4 paper
a paper clip

Basic paper plane

1. Fold a sheet of paper as shown in the pictures.

2. Throw it across the room several times to see how it flies.

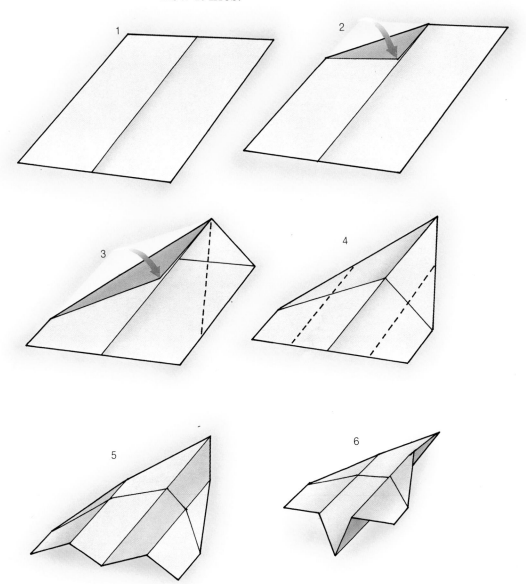

3. Now alter the way your plane flies by changing its shape.

4. Bend up the back edges of the wings, and see if it makes a difference. If you throw the plane hard, does it shoot up right away? What happens if you throw it gently?

Pitch down paper plane

Bend the wings' edges down, and fly it again. Now what happens? Can you see what effect the bent edges are having on the plane's flight? When you bent the edges up, the plane tried to rise. Bending them down makes it dive.

Rolling left and right

Now see what happens when you bend one side up and the other one down.

One wing tries to go up. The other wing tries to go down. Because the wings are attached to each other, the plane tilts, or rolls. Depending on which flap is up and which is down, the plane rolls left or right.

Which way did your plane roll? Reverse the bent edges and see if it rolls the other way.

1. Flatten your plane's wings again or make a new one.

2. Slide a paper clip on to the nose of the plane before you fly it. Does it still fly well? Which direction does it want to go?

3. Move the paper clip to the back end. What happens now?

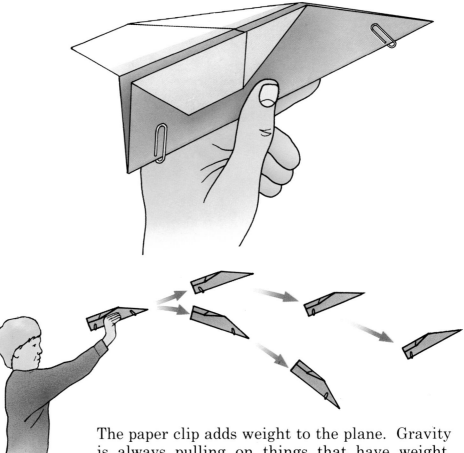

The paper clip adds weight to the plane. Gravity is always pulling on things that have weight. When the paper clip is on the front of the plane, gravity is pulling down more on the nose. So the plane dives. When the paper clip is at the back, gravity pulls down more on the rear of the plane. Then the plane tries to fly by lifting its nose.

A hovercraft is a machine that floats on a cushion of air. You can build a hovercraft yourself. It will glide around a table top or across the floor.

1. Glue the large end of a cork to the centre of the bottom of a polystyrene food tray.

2. When the glue is dry, make a hole through the cork and tray with the nail. The nail is sharp – be very careful with it. After you make the hole, be sure that the cork is still glued securely to the tray.

3. Set the hovercraft on a table top or on a smooth, hard floor. Blow up a balloon. Put the mouth of the balloon over the narrow end of the cork and let it go. If your hovercraft doesn't take off immediately, give it a nudge.

You will need
1 cork
a polystyrene food tray
a thin nail
non-toxic glue
a balloon

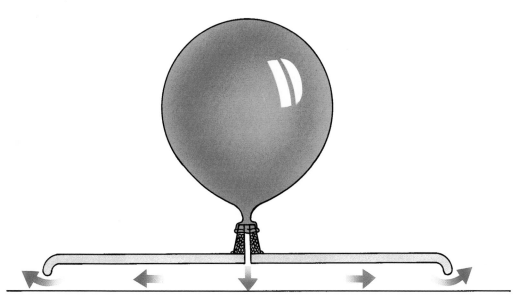

The air rushing out of the balloon spreads out under the tray and lifts it. The hovercraft floats on the cushion of air underneath it. See how easily it can change direction. How far can it go with just a small nudge?

Helicopter

To fly, an aeroplane must move forward at great speed. It needs lots of air speeding over its wings to create lift. A helicopter, however, can remain in one place and still create all the lift it needs. It spins its "wings", called rotors, round in a circle. This lifts the craft and enables it to fly in any direction.

You will need

stiff card
tape
1 piece of dowelling that
   fits in a cotton reel,
   10-15cm (4-6in) long
1 cotton reel
string

1. Use the diagram to cut out a set of rotors. First cut an equilateral triangle from stiff card. Trace the diagram below and carefully transfer the lines on to the card triangle.

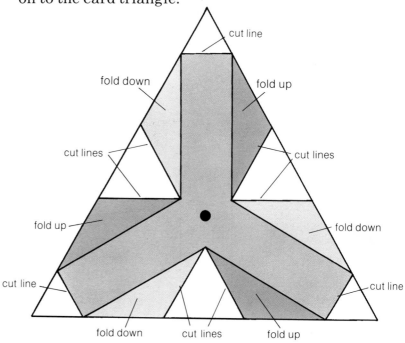

2. Cut a hole in the centre of the rotors. Make the hole slightly smaller than the dowelling.

3. Wrap tape thickly but neatly round the dowelling about 0·5cm (¼in) from one end to form a collar.

4. Put the short end of the stick through the centre hole in the rotors. Twist it gently until the collar fits snugly against the card.

5. Tape the end of the dowelling sticking through the top of the card to the rotors.

6. Bend all the rotors as shown. Make them look like the picture. Be sure not to tear any of them.

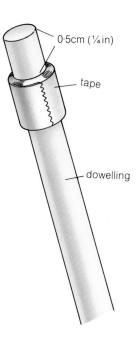

0·5cm (¼in)

tape

dowelling

7. Place the stick in the hole of the cotton reel. Wind a string round the stick.

8. Pull on the string hard to make the helicopter's rotor blades spin rapidly. The helicopter should lift up and fly out of the cotton reel.

Repeat the experiment, but this time tilt the cotton reel a bit. Does the helicopter now fly forward as well as up?

Orbiting Ball

Hundreds of satellites are orbiting the Earth all the time. They are held in place by gravity. Some are only a few hundred kilometres up. Many are as much as 50,000 kilometres high. Satellites must fly through space at just the right speed. If satellites flew at the wrong speeds, gravity would pull them back to Earth.

You will need

2 paper clips
a piece of smooth, strong string (waxed dental floss, fishing line or similar), 1m (1 yd) long
125g (5oz) of plasticine
a large cotton reel

1. Twist two paper clips into rough shapes. (The exact shape is not important.)

2. Slip the floss through the cotton reel. Tie a paper clip to each end of the floss.

3. Stick a lump of plasticine around each paper clip. Make the first lump into a ball weighing about 25g (1oz). Make the second lump about 100g (4oz).

4. Hold the cotton reel with the smaller lump of clay on top. Spin the reel to make the top lump swing round. Try not to let the line rub against your hand. Swing the plasticine in a circle quickly. You will see it spin outwards, away from the reel. As the small lump moves further out, it needs to spin slower and slower to hold the larger lump steady.

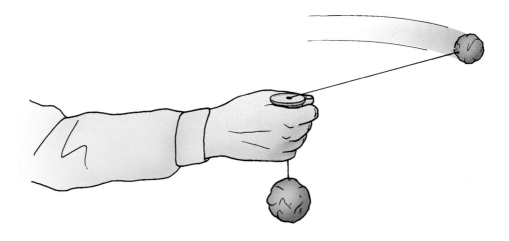

The larger lump is always pulling down on the line. It is trying to pull the smaller lump back to the reel. Its pull is constant, like the pull of gravity. It does not matter whether the small lump is near the spool or far away from it. The larger lump still has the same pull on the line. The spinning lump holds the large lump in place.

SATELLITES
In 1957 the Soviet Union launched Sputnik, the world's first artificial satellite. Since then, many nations have launched hundreds of satellites.
Each satellite is designed to do a single job. Many satellites monitor the weather. Others are used for communication, navigation, or scientific study.

Rocket Balloon

Real rockets cannot be kept in line on a string! They have fins to help them fly straight. Without fins, a rocket would zoom off in any direction.

You will need
a long balloon
heavy paper
scissors
tape

1. Cut four paper triangles as shown from heavy paper. Fold one edge of each triangle at right angles. These triangles will be the fins for your balloon rocket.

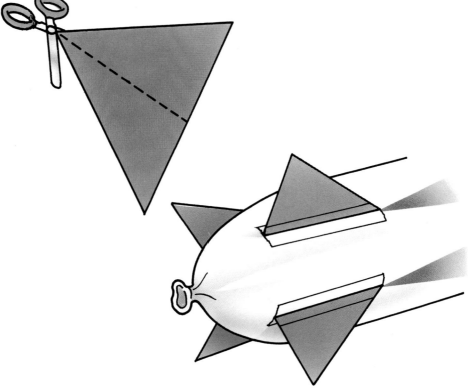

2. Blow up the balloon about half way. This will make it easier to attach the fins. Get a parent, teacher or friend to hold the neck of the balloon shut for you with their fingers. Do not tie the neck.

3. Tape the fins around the back end of your balloon. Try to space them equally.

4. Blow up the balloon the rest of the way. Pinch the neck shut yourself. Hold the balloon rocket upright. Launch it by letting go and watch your rocket fly.

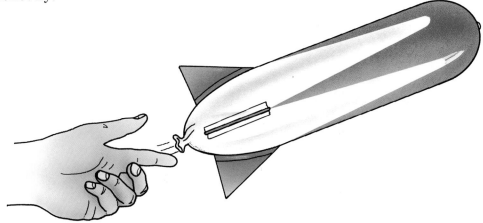

Does your rocket with fins fly straighter than the ordinary balloon rocket on pages 10 and 11 did?

ROCKETS

Today's giant, complicated rockets have ancient ancestors. The Chinese invented rockets, probably in the 13th century. The first ones were not much more than large fireworks, but they terrified the opponents of the Chinese warriors.

Six hundred years later, the British developed an improved version of larger rockets with explosive warheads. They used them against the Americans in the War of 1812. The Americans used rockets during the Civil War. Rockets were used by the Germans in World War II and in more recent times rockets have been used to launch satellites into space and put men onto the moon.

Launch Your Own Rocket

You can launch a rocket by squeezing air to make it fly. A real rocket moves because hot, fast gases from burning fuel rush out of the back end of the rocket. The rocket responds by flying forward.

You will need

2 straws (one big enough to slide over the other)
an empty washing-up liquid bottle
glue
card
tape
plasticine

1. Glue a thin straw to the nozzle of the cap on an empty washing-up liquid bottle. Pack some plasticine around the base of the straw where it joins the cap. This will help seal it.

2. Cut out three cardboard triangles. Tape them to one end of the thick straw. They are the rocket's fins.

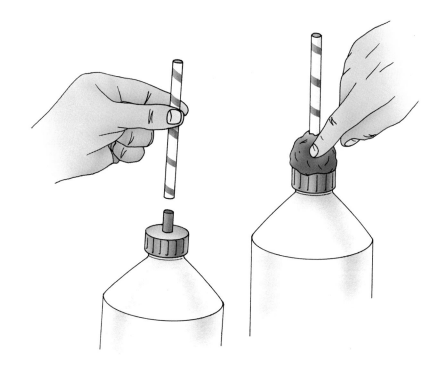

3. Give your rocket a nose cone of plasticine. Make sure it is firmly in place.

4. Slide your rocket over the thin straw on the squeezy bottle. Let the thin straw poke very lightly into the plasticine nose cone.

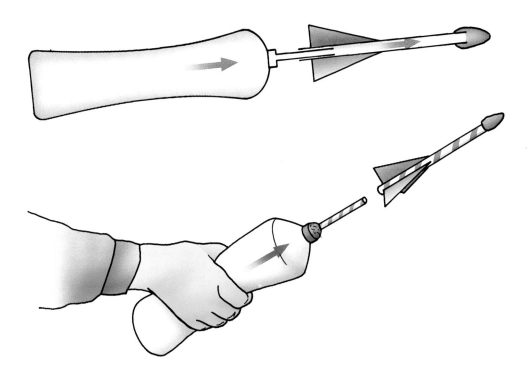

5. Give the bottle a quick, hard squeeze. Watch your rocket leap into the air.

Squeezing the bottle forces air into the rocket just below the nose cone. This air must get out some-how. The only exit available is from the back of the rocket. Air rushing out of the back makes your rocket fly forward, just like a real one.

Safety Notes

The projects and experiments in this book are designed to show how certain principles of science work. Most of them are simple to do. Some of them should not be done without permission from an adult. These experiments are marked with this symbol:

It is a good idea to ask permission in any case. You should also make sure that an adult is available to answer any questions that you have.

Some projects are marked with the symbol: (A)

DO NOT TRY TO DO THESE UNLESS YOU HAVE AN ADULT
AVAILABLE TO HELP YOU.

Good scientists are very careful. They always protect themselves and other people. They listen to good advice. If you follow the rules given here, you should always stay safe.

Starting work
Before you begin, read the instructions. This will help you understand what must be done. Read the list of materials that you need. Collect everything on the list and put it in one place before you start. Some experiments need some preparation, such as cutting things out or measuring and weighing. Do this first. Remember to get permission if you need it.

Heat, fire and electricity
Some of the projects may involve the use of heat or a flame. Anything that is hot can burn you. Never play with fire, heat or electricity.

Remember that fire is always dangerous. Always ask an adult to help with experiments in which you need to use a cooker or the flame from a candle. Use only safety matches. Place all your materials so that you do not need to reach across a flame. Do not wear loose clothing that could accidentally get caught in the flame. Keep a pail or jug of water close by just in case.

If you are using electricity, always ask an adult to keep an eye on you. Remember that mains electricity can kill.

Sharp edges
Some of the projects may involve the use of scissors or knives. Objects with sharp edges are dangerous. Always ask an adult to help with these experiments. Get them to cut out things that you need for a project. Be very careful when opening tins or using mirrors.

Remember that glass breaks easily and broken glass has sharp edges. Most of the projects can be done using plastic jars and glasses. If you do break a glass, get someone to help clear it up immediately.

Chemicals

Some of the projects may involve the use of chemicals. All the chemicals used in this book are harmless household substances, but all chemicals should be treated with respect. Make sure that all containers of chemicals are labelled clearly. Keep them out of the reach of small children and inquisitive animals. Never mix chemical substances unless you are sure that you know what will happen. Some harmless chemicals can become dangerous when they are mixed together. Make sure that you dispose of your chemicals when you have finished the experiment. Wrap dry substances in old newspaper and throw them away. Pour liquids down the sink or an outside drain and flush them away thoroughly with plenty of clean water.

Tools and equipment

Tools such as hammers and nails or drills can cause injury. Always ask an adult for help if you need to use tools in an experiment. They can help you nail or glue things together or drill holes or cut things out.

General rules for safe science

* If in doubt, ask for help from an adult.
* Always wash your hands before you start and when you finish.
* Cover your work surface with old newspapers to protect it.
* Never do any experiment without careful planning. Never try an experiment just to see what will happen.
* You can collect useful objects such as empty containers, card or paper, pencils, etc, to help you in your experiments. Always make sure they are clean. Store them neatly in a convenient place.
* It is a good idea to keep a notebook of your experiments. Take notes after you have done an experiment. Your notes will be useful in the future. If you find that an experiment does not work, your notes will help you understand why. Then you can try the experiment again.
* Always clear everything up after you have finished your experiment. Put away any materials that are left and put any equipment that you have used back where it belongs. Throw away any rubbish.
* Keep dangerous objects and substances out of the reach of smaller children and animals.

Words to Remember

accelerate going faster and faster

air pressure the weight of air pushing down on an object

canopy the "umbrella" part of a parachute

compress to squeeze together

dive a rapid movement towards the ground

drag any force on a flying machine that reduces its forward speed

fin a stiff triangle at the rear of a rocket that helps it to fly straight

gas an invisible collection of certain kinds of molecules that can move freely in all directions

glide flying without power or floating in air in a controlled way

gravity the force which makes an object fall towards Earth

helium a kind of gas that is even lighter than air

lift any force on a flying machine that makes it go up

molecule a tiny particle of matter made up of even smaller bits called atoms

orbit the path of a satellite zooming round the Earth

parachute a cloth or other soft sheet made for the purpose of lowering a person or object gently to the ground

roll the tilting of a flying machine to the left or right

rotor the spinning blades on top of a helicopter that give it lift

satellite a body in orbit round a planet

thrust any force on a flying machine that makes it go forward

vent the hole in the top of a parachute's canopy through which air escapes

Books to Read

The Story of the Space Shuttle by Tim Furniss Hodder & Stoughton 1979
Early Aircraft Collins 1977
Aviation by Gottfried Hilscher Junior Knowledge Series, Lutterworth Press 1972
The World's Helicopters by Joan Bradbrooke The Bodley Head 1972
Aviation: The Complete Book of Aircraft and Flight Octopus Books 1980
Flight Life Science Library, Time Inc 1973
Flight and Floating by Alan Ward Usborne Books 1981
Jets Usborne Young Scientist Series 1978
Spaceflight Usborne Young Scientist Series 1978
Airliners Franklin Watts 1989
Aircraft by Robin Kerrod Franklin Watts 1977
Helicopters Franklin Watts 1989
Helicopters by Graham Rickard Wayland Books 1987
Helicopters by J P Rutland Franklin Watts 1979
Helicopters by David Jefferis Franklin Watts 1987
Hovercraft by Angela Croome Hodder & Stoughton 1984
The Hovercraft by E S Hayden Ladybird Books 1979
The Story of Flight by Jim Robins Piccolo 1986
The Paper Airplane Book by Seymour Simon Puffin Books 1971
The Science Book by Sara Stein Heinemann 1979
The All Year Round series by Kathleen Edwards Macdonald 1987
Why Things Are general editor Lesley Firth Kingfisher Books 1989
Beginning to Learn about Science by Richard L Allington PhD and Kathleen Krull Blackwell Raintree Ltd 1983
Simple Science Experiments by Eiji and Masako Orii Gareth Stevens Children's Books 1989
Illustrated Science Dictionary Longman 1981
Science for Life by Bishop, Maddocks and Scott Collins Educational 1984
Airliners by Bill Gunston Granada 1982

Index